The Adventures of Jake Skater

by Devon Raney

Illustrated by Aaron Reid

Copyright

The Raney Group LLC
Printed in Washington on recycled paper.

by Devon Raney
Illustrated by Aaron Reid

For my beautiful daughter Madrona, and our family friend Cannon, who both served as an inspiration for this character.

Much thanks to Dave Raney for typing the words when my eyes have failed me, and for his editorial skills.

Thank you to everyone below who took time to read the book and give me feedback. Most importantly, thank you to Rebecca whose patience is immeasurable. Pam, Laura, Blake, Chanda, Taylor, Landen, Alder, Larry, Robin, Gabby, Miss Peg, Miss Caroline, Temple, Barrett, Ayla, Mike, Tom, Verna, Ron, Aaron, Shane, Corena, Abbey, Luke, Emily, Lydia, Tom B., Dave, Brandon, George S., Lars, Cressa, Cannon and Madrona.

Jake Johnson loved to play sports. The only problem was that he was smaller than most other kids.

Like a small stick on a swift creek, Jake went wherever the day took him. In the town of Trellis Bay where Jake lived, this was not hard to do. He spent his days with his dog Sam combing the beaches at low tide for butter clam shells, gooey ducks, razor clams and Dungeness crab.

He and Sam always watched in amazement as seagulls picked up clams, flew high into the air and dropped them onto the pavement below, trying to crack them open for food. Jake laughed out loud when the occasional seagull dropped a clam on a car roof.

"dink!"

Sometimes in the cool evenings, Jake and Sam sat on the dock and watched salmon popping out of the water. Jake enjoyed the fresh salmon meals his mom made whenever they caught one.

Jake's adventures, however, were always interrupted by the dinner bell his mom rang to bring them home. But on this particular day when they heard the bell, Jake said to Sam, "Let's get home quickly tonight. Tomorrow's my birthday."

Jake popped up on a sunny Saturday morning, tore out of his room and, looking for his dad, found him in the kitchen. He yelled excitedly,

"Whaaaat's uuuuup Daaaaad!"

Jake's mom was whipping the eggs, his older brother Ronnie (who'd be leaving for college soon) was filling four glasses with orange juice and Jake's dad was setting the table while humming to his favorite country music that played in the background.

"Throw some salmon on those eggs!" Jake yelled, delirious with all the excitement. Once they'd finished eating, Jake, who was stuffed to the brim and smiling, eagerly awaited what all kids know is the best part...the presents.

The loot was worthy. Jake's mom presented him with football cleats and back to school clothes. His dad gave him a fancy rain slicker and backpack with more compartments than Jake would know what to do with. But it was Ronnie's present that was the real surprise. Always in awe of his older brother, Jake was amazed to open Ronnie's present and find a brand new skateboard.

"Summer always goes by too quickly," Jake said to Sam as he buttoned up his new flannel shirt. In a morning daze that was uncharacteristic of Jake's usual enthusiasm, he stared blankly into his closet — first at his skateboard, which he had not yet ridden, then at his cleats, which he had not yet worn.

"Jake!" his mom yelled from the hallway. "You're almost late for your first day of school. Come on, let's roll." Grabbing his backpack, Jake ran to the car and loaded up for the short ride to school.

Turning, the two boys stared up at the big brick building — Bay Ridge Elementary School. It seemed like a mile of steps leading up to the front door. Classrooms on one side of the school had large windows that opened up to the bay, while those on the other side had views of the Bay Ridge athletic fields. Jake had hoped this year he would be in a classroom with a bay view. So he was disappointed when he realized that he and his fellow classmates had a premium view of...the football field.

Jake was stoked when he saw his dad and Sam waiting for him outside school to take the shortcut home. He barely got in a "hello" before handing over the football sign-up sheet and beginning a nearly incoherent ramble about his first day at school.

When they reached the wooded trail that was their shortcut home, Jake took the leash off Sam so they could run the rest of the way. "It's tough to tell who's going to win this race," Jake's dad thought to himself, grinning, as Jake broke out ahead of the muscular retriever.

It became obvious that Jake's small stature had not affected his athleticism. He seemed to run and jump without even looking at the obstacles around him, leaping over downed trees and boosting one-footed airs off tree stumps. Each new stride seemed to be led by the movement of Jake's hands and supported by the lean muscles in his arms and legs.

Having always known first-hand Jake's high energy level, his dad in that moment became even more keenly aware of his son's athletic ability. Smiling again, he took off himself, trying to catch up with Jake and Sam. By the time he did, they were already at the front door of their house. Laughing out loud, he picked Jake up, hugged him and said, "Man, you're getting fast!"

Jake went into his room. He placed his schoolbooks on his desk and his backpack in the closet...between the skateboard he'd not yet ridden, and the cleats he had not yet worn.

On Saturday, it was back to the trail and up to the Bay Ridge football fields for Jake and his dad.

"It was a different time when I grew up," Jake's dad said. "No cell phones. No laptops. No video games."

"Yeah, Dad, and only three sports, right? Football, basketball and baseball?"

Jake's dad laughed out loud.

"Yeah, and we walked to school uphill both ways...AND in the snow."

Laughing together, they rounded a bend in the trail and came upon the chaotic circus frenzy that was the football tryouts.

"There are a lot of people," Jake said, looking around the crowded field with wide eyes. "A lot of these kids aren't from Bay Ridge."

"Let's go to the sign up tent," his dad said. Jake scanned the team assignments and saw that Tommy's team — the Seahawks — was already full.

Jake was assigned to the Buccaneers and told to go see Coach Darrell Riggins under a white banner at the north end of the field. He said goodbye to his dad and took his place in line. The Buccaneers were running cone drills, each player weaving back and forth over the 15-yard course, and then returning to the line.

Jake wasn't hard to spot. He was at least a foot shorter than all of the other players. And teams were taking kids that were nine, ten and eleven years old, so Jake was also one of the youngest out there.

"You're darned fast, Johnson!" yelled Coach Riggins. Jake knew that it was true. He had been first in all three of the speed and agility drills. He ran the cones faster than anybody, he was yards ahead in the sprints and he caught everything thrown to him in the passing drills.

"Okay everybody," Coach Riggins whistled, "it's time to get the pads and helmets on." Helmets were laid out in boxes by size and naturally Jake went to find an extra small one. The one he selected didn't fit, not even close. It was so loose he could spin it 360 degrees around his head — even with the chinstrap buckled. He chuckled out loud. "This is how an owl must feel," he thought.

Leaving it on, he took his place in line. During the sprints, Coach Riggins watched in horror as Jake's helmet sagged down over his eyes and he ran head first into the sign up tent and knocked over a water cooler. Jake's facemask slammed down on his nose abruptly during the collision, and he had a pretty good nosebleed going as he picked himself up. Jake's dad was there to help.

As he was taking off his pads, he heard his new coach say, "Mr. Johnson, I'd like a word with you!" He overheard the gruff coach's voice — "Your son is the fastest one out there, but this may not be the year for him..."

"It's Tuesday afternoon," Jake thought sluggishly. "Three days since tryouts." He stared into his closet at his cleats. There was still dried blood on them from Saturday's gigantic helmet incident. He kicked his cleats aside and made room for his backpack. He caught a glimpse of his skateboard; there was nothing on it, not even a scratch. He turned around and stared at his dog.

"Did you know that Tommy already got his equipment?" he said to Sam. "A brand new silver helmet. Brand new pads." Sam looked up at Jake, his ears down and tail wagging excitedly. And Jake knew exactly what Sam was saying. "You're right, Sam. We should go do something fun. Let's run as fast as we can to the city park and I'll find you the biggest stick in the world."

Jake walked for a while in a trance, remembering what had happened over the past few days. Then, all of a sudden, he didn't know where they were. Jake's imagination began to run wild. This was unfamiliar territory. The sounds of the highway and Jake's neighborhood had faded. Sam had stopped dead in his tracks. Without knowing why, or perhaps for some magical reason in some magical place, all Jake wanted to do was walk further.

"Where are we Sam?"

No sooner had he said those words than they came up out of the woods at the edge of the skate park.

"Wow Sam, we must have gotten lost. We're at the opposite end of the city park. Look, there's the playground and swing set way over there. How did we get so spun around?"

This mysterious path had led him to a world entirely new to him. He watched in amazement as the skateboarders painted invisible lines on the walls and angles of this awesome concrete landscape.

Jake popped up out of bed. "I dreamt all night about skateboarding, Mom!"

He threw on his clothes, brushed his teeth, grabbed his backpack and, this time, he brought his skateboard too...all before jumping in the car for the ride to school.

"I'm going to spend all afternoon at the skate park, if that's okay, Mom."

She laughed and replied, **"All** afternoon, Jake?"

"Yeah, that's right, **all** afternoon." And he gave her a kiss as he opened the door and jumped out onto the curb.

School flew by that day for Jake. And his studies probably suffered as he began drawing pictures of all things skateboarding.

That day's final school bell didn't sound like the final bell it usually did to Jake. As soon it rang, Jake began to visualize the path to the mysterious new world he had landed on the day before. He scanned the tree line, looking for clues that would lead him to the trail... then he saw it. Walking slowly between the two tall fir trees, he ran up the trail to repeat the magic.

"Is this your first time skating?"

Embarrassed, Jake looked up and saw an older skater who was suddenly standing nearby. "Hey, you're Ronnie's brother aren't you?" Jake nodded and said yes. "All right, why don't you just start down there in the flat bottom," and he pointed into the middle of the park where the ramps and bowls flattened out to make level ground. "You skate up those walls the best you can and try to come down backwards; skaters call that 'fakie.' If you get that done today, Jake, you can try something new tomorrow. I'll make sure everyone stays out of your way. You just keep going up and down the walls."

The news came to Jake through his dad. There were no football helmets small enough to fit his head. It would not be his year for football.

Jake didn't care. Tommy had come by two days before and surprised him. "I know you've been skating all the time," Tommy said, "and I want you to have this skateboard helmet." It meant the world to Jake. He had made a lot of new friends at the skate park but still loved hanging out with Tommy.

Every time Jake put the helmet on it was like putting on a space suit that carried him into orbit and took him to that magical world once again.

Jake's weeks went by quickly, turning into months.

Jake seemed excited at school, actually enjoying his projects and fully engaging in his lessons. He knew that at the end of day he was going to run home, grab his skateboard and race to the skate park.

On one particular day, Jake was pushing his skateboard by the football field when he stopped and stared at his friends and peers while they were practicing. He wondered why he didn't miss this camaraderie. Filled with an overwhelming desire to share his excitement and energy, he shouted "do good in practice today, Tommy!"

As Jake again headed towards the skate park he heard some of the older kids snickering and one of them said out loud, "There goes Jake Johnson," while another piped up quite loudly, "Don't you mean Jake the Skater!"

Jake stopped again, thinking about the remark. He turned in the older boy's direction with a smile and yelled as loudly as he could, "That's right, I am Jake Skater," and pushing his board down the sidewalk he ollied off the curb in front of the crowd of players.

One evening, Jake returned home from the skate park to find the energy quite upbeat. His parents were in an exceptionally good mood.

"What's going on?" Jake asked.

Over a fresh cooked homemade meal, his parents told him his brother Ronnie would be coming home for Thanksgiving dinner that Thursday.

Jake was more than excited; this was the culmination of all he had been secretly working on since summer. He was going to share his magical world with Ronnie.

The temperature had dropped to the low 50s and the rain stopped for two whole days.

Jake suddenly woke up. It was Thursday morning and Ronnie was already cooking breakfast with their mom.

"Hey Ronnie," Jake said.

"Hey there Jake," Ronnie replied, "Mom says you've been skating everyday at the park after school."

Jake laughed. "It's MY world up there now, Ronnie."

Ronnie returned the laugh, secretly remembering when he felt the same way.

"That sounds great, Jake, we'll go up there and skate as soon as we're done eating."

Jake inhaled his turkey and gravy, with the eager anticipation of skating with his older brother.